LATIN ROCKS ON

LATIN
ROCKS

SARAH ROWLEY

UNICORN

Published in 2020 by Unicorn, an imprint
of Unicorn Publishing Group LLP
5 Newburgh Street
London, W1F 7RG
www.unicornpublishing.org

ISBN 978-1-912690-87-9
10 9 8 7 6 5 4 3 2 1

Design by Anna Hopwood

CONTENTS

Introduction

THE IDEA FOR THIS BOOK originated from the Twitter handle @LatinRocksON that I set up with my sister in order to bring my two passions together: the Latin language and pop music. I stumbled across the idea of translating pop lyrics into Latin after I had had yet another conversation (monologue) attempting to convince a friend of the continued importance and relevance of the Classics, specifically the Latin language. Studying Latin has given me so much joy over the years, and I was determined to share it with other people in an accessible and hopefully less daunting form. Music is the ultimate unifier, so I decided to start translating pop lyrics into Latin on Twitter and ask people to guess the singer and song. From there, @LatinRocksON was born.

Over the years @LatinRocksON has covered lyrics from U2 to Smokey Robinson, Beyoncé to Bruce Springsteen. It has gained a fantastic and diverse following in that time, not least the school teachers in America who told me that they quiz their pupils on a different lyric at the beginning of every lesson. Where possible I recreated the natural melody or hook of a song if it was really well-known, at times sacrificing grammatical prowess in favour of the greater artistic endeavour!

In compiling this collection I was lucky enough to work with several prominent Classicists whose expertise has made these modern lyrics as historically accurate and authentic as possible. I have also added punctuation to the Latin so as to better reflect the English – knowing that the Romans didn't work with punctuation, this addition is intended more as a translation guide than anything else. I had a similar objective when grouping the artists thematically by musical genre or era, so readers may have different opinions on where to put them. I hope you enjoy the book as much as I enjoyed creating the translations. If you have any suggestions for more lyrics to add, tweet me @LatinRocksON – *mirabile dictu*!

Icons

equi indomiti non
mihi abstrahant.
equi indomiti
indomiti –
equitabimus
postmodum.

Wild horses couldn't
drag me away.
Wild, wild horses –
we'll ride them
someday.

The Rolling Stones, *Wild Horses*

**quod tu velis, care, id habeo...
quod tu requiras,
scisne quomodo ego id acceperim?
rogo modo... parvam reverentiam.**

What you want... Baby I got (ooo)
What you need (ooo)... Do you know how I got it?
All I'm asking for... is a little respect.

Aretha Franklin, *Respect*

**sorores id faciunt pro ipsis... stantes
in suis duobus pedibus et personantes
sua tintinnabula...**

Sisters are doin' it for themselves... standing on their
own two feet, and ringing on their own bells...

Aretha Franklin & The Eurythmics, *Sisters Are Doin' It for Themselves*

**amicula, permitto tibi vehere meum
currum. ita vero ero persona celebris.
amicula, permitto tibi vehere meum
currum. et fortasse te amabo...**

Baby, you can drive my car. Yes I'm gonna be a star. Baby,
you can drive my car. And maybe I'll love you...

The Beatles, *Drive My Car*

Lucia (est) in caelo cum gemmis...
Lucia in caelo cum gemmis...

Lucy in the sky with diamonds...
Lucy in the sky with diamonds...

The Beatles, *Lucy in the Sky with Diamonds*

domine aut domina, legesne meum libellum? absumpsi multos annos scribendo. visne videre?

Dear Sir or Madam, will you read my book?
It took me years to write, will you take a look?

The Beatles, *Paperback Writer*

tu eris semper pars mei, sum pars tui in perpetuum. nonne scis te non posse me evadere, care, quia tu eris semper mi care.

You'll always be a part of me, I'm part of
you indefinitely. Boy don't you know
you can't escape me. Oooh darling 'cause
you'll always be my baby.

Mariah Carey, *Always Be My Baby*

**unus amor, una vita... cum est
unum opus, in media nocte.**

One love, one life... when it's one
need, in the night.

U2, *One*

**unus homo venit in nomine amoris. unus
venit et discessit. unus venit ut approbaret.
unus venit ut superaret. in nomine amoris!**

One man come in the name of love,
one man come and go.
One man come he to justify.
One man to overthrow.
In the name of love!

U2, *Pride (In the Name of Love)*

**tu non potes commovere ignem,
tu non potes commovere ignem sine
scintilla. hoc telum conducendum
ut saltemus in tenebris.**

You can't start a fire, you can't start a fire
without a spark. This gun's for hire even if we
are just dancing in the dark.

Bruce Springsteen, *Dancing in the Dark*

tu es tam vanus…
ut tu putes id
carmen de te esse.
tu es tam vanus…
ut iurem te putare id
carmen de te esse.

You're so vain… you
prob'ly think this song
is about you. You're so
vain… I bet you think this
song is about you.

Carly Simon, *You're So Vain*

pisces in mare, scitis quomodo sentiam. flumen fluens libenter, scis quomodo sentiam. est mihi aurora nova, est dies nova, est vita nova...

Fish in the sea, you know how I feel. River running free you know how I feel. It's a new dawn, it's a new day, it's a new life for me...

Nina Simone, *Feeling Good*

ego debeo habere fidem, ego debeo habere fidem. care, scio te rogare me ut maneam. dic, quaeso quaeso quaeso – noli abire!

'Cause I gotta have faith, I gotta have faith. Baby! I know you're asking me to stay. Say please please please don't go away!

George Michael, *Faith*

fortasse sum similis patris mei, nimis superbus. fortasse tu es similis matris meae, illa est numquam contenta.

Maybe I'm just like my father, too demanding. Maybe you're just like my mother, she's never satisfied.

Prince, *When Doves Cry*

favillae ad favillas, mirificus ad mirificum.
certo scimus Imperatorem Tom-mem
esse toxicomaniacum.

Ashes to ashes, funk to funky.
We know
Major Tom's a junkie.

David Bowie, *Ashes to Ashes*

saltemus! indue tuos calceos rubros et
salta ad rhythmum! saltemus!

Let's dance! Put on your red shoes and
dance the blues! Let's dance!

David Bowie, *Let's Dance*

est haec vita vera?
est simpliciter somnium?
captivus in vortice non fugio
a realitate..!

Is this the real life?
Is this just fantasy?
Caught in a landslide, no escape
from reality…!

Queen, *Bohemian Rhapsody*

pecunia, pecunia, pecunia oblectatio esse debet, in mundo hominis divitis.

Money, money, money must be funny, in the rich man's world.

Abba, *Money, Money, Money*

**tu es saltans regina, iuvenis et dulcis,
modo septemdecim, saltans regina!
senti modum tympani...**

You are the dancing queen, young and sweet,
only seventeen. Dancing queen! Feel the beat
from the tambourine…

Abba, *Dancing Queen*

**est magna dissimilitudo inter nos...
et milia milia passuum...
salve ab altera parte!**

There's such a difference between us and
a million miles… hello from the other side!

Adele, *Hello*

**vidi lumen vidi lumen.
non plus tenebrae, non plus nox.
nunc ego sum tam laetus...
est nullus dolor in visu.**

I saw the light, I saw the light.
No more darkness, no more night.
Now I'm so happy… no sorry in sight.

Hank Williams, *I Saw the Light*

ego volo evadere! ego volo evadere tua mendacia, tu es tam superbus ego te non requiro. deus cognoscit, ego volo evadere.

I want to break free! I want to break free from your lies, you're so self-satisfied, I don't need you. God knows, I want to break free.

Queen, *I Want To Break Free*

ad sinistrum, ad sinistrum. omnia quae tu possides sunt in arco ad sinistrum. in vestiario meae res sunt – si eas emi, te oro, noli tangere!

To the left, to the left. Everything you own in the box to the left. In the closet, that's my stuff, yes if I bought it, please don't touch!

Beyoncé, *Irreplaceable*

bibi, bibi… ebria in amore, te volo… ebria in amore…

I've been drinkin', I've been drinkin'… drunk in love. I want you… drunk in love…

Beyoncé, *Drunk In Love*

vita est ambages,
necesse est
omnibus stare
solis. audio te
meum nomen
appellare.

Life is a mystery,
everyone must
stand alone.
I hear you
call my name.

Madonna, *Like a Prayer*

cara puta iterum, nostri amoris et memoriae causa, puta iterum ignis et fidei causa qui tibi et mihi attigerunt. cara, hoc est grave...

Baby think twice, for the sake of our love,
for our memory, for the fire and the faith that
was you and me. Baby this is serious...

Celine Dion, *Think Twice*

estne in eius oculis? eheu! tu falleris. estne in eius suspiriis? eheu! simulabit. si vis noscere utrum te amet, est in eius osculo!

Is it in his eyes? Oh no you'll be deceived.
Is it in his sighs? Oh no, he'll make believe.
If you want to know if he loves you so, it's in his kiss.

Cher, *The Shoop Shoop Song (It's in His Kiss)*

es simpliciter optimus... melior ceteris omnibus!

You're simply the best...
better than all the rest!

Tina Turner, *The Best*

ocule auris, eius debilitatem inveni.
ocule auris, faciet quod velim…

GoldenEye, I found his weakness.
GoldenEye, he'll do what I please…

Tina Turner, *GoldenEye*

ego odi imbrem in meam fenestram,
dulces memorias revocantem…

I can't stand the rain, against my window,
bringing back sweet memories…

Tina Turner, *I Can't Stand the Rain*

magna rota, perge vertere! Maria
Magnifica, perge fervere!
verte, verte, verte in flumine!

Big wheel, keep on turnin'!
Proud Mary, keep on burnin'!
Rollin', rollin', rollin' on the river!

Tina Turner, *Proud Mary*

**audio infantes lacrimantes,
video eos crescere. et ego cogito...
"o mundum mirabilem!"**

I hear babies crying, I watch them grow.
And I think to myself…
'what a wonderful world!'

Louis Armstrong, *What a Wonderful World*

**mea mater mihi dixit, te non posse
festinare amorem. necesse est manere...
esse lusum ad dandum et accipiendum.**

My Mama said, you can't hurry love. No you
just have to wait… it's a game of give and take.

Phil Collins, *You Can't Hurry Love*

**tu vides tantum quod tui oculi
volunt videre. quomodo vita potest
esse quod tu velis id esse?
gelata es cum cor tuum non patet.**

You only see what your eyes want to see.
How can life be what you want it to be?
You're frozen, when your heart's not open.

Madonna, *Frozen*

**similis virginis, tactae primo tempore.
similis virginis, cum pectus
tuum pulsat prope meum.**

Like a virgin, touched for the very first time.
Like a virgin, when your heart
beats next to mine.

Madonna, *Like A Virgin*

**quod sum malus, sum malus, valde
valde malus. et orbis terrarum debet
respondere statim… quis est malus?**

Because I'm bad, I'm bad, really really bad.
And the whole world has to answer right now…
who's bad?

Michael Jackson, *Bad*

**Layla, sum in genibus tibi. Layla, te oro,
cara, te quaeso. Layla, cara, levabisne
meam mentem sollicitam?**

Layla, you've got me on my knees. Layla, I'm begging,
darling please. Layla, darling, won't you ease
my worried mind?

Eric Clapton, *Layla*

**necesse est nobis abire
dum sumus adulescentes,
quod mendici
adsimiles nobis,
amicula – nati sumus
ut curramus.**

We gotta get out while
we're young,
'cause tramps like us,
baby – we were born to run.

Bruce Springsteen, *Born to Run*

**est forma veneficii,
est forma veneficii.
unum somnium, unus animus,
unum pretium.**

It's a kind of magic, it's a kind of magic.
One dream, one soul, one prize.

Queen, *A Kind of Magic*

ego sum vir missilis… et ego credo id futurum esse diu.

I'm a rocket man… and I think it's gonna be a long, long time.

Elton John, *Rocket Man*

The 80s

aurum! (aurum!) semper crede in tuo animo. tu habes auctoritatem scire te indissolubilem esse!

Gold! (Gold!)
Always believe in your
soul. You've got the
power to know,
you're indestructible!

Spandau Ballet, *Gold*

illa habet risum qui (videtur) revocat memoriam iuventutis, ubi omnia erant tam viridia quam caelum caeruleum. eheu! o mi dulcis infans!

She's got a smile that it seems to me, reminds me of childhood memories, Where everything was as fresh as the bright blue sky.
Oh oh oh! Sweet child o' mine!

Guns N' Roses, *Sweet Child O' Mine*

illa id habet! ita vero cara, illa id habet! sum Venus tua, sum tua flamma, quae est tua cupiditas?

She's got it! Yeah baby, she's got it! I'm your Venus, I'm your fire, what's your desire?

Bananarama, *Venus*

vah! sumus in medio itinere, vah! vivimus in prece. cape manum meam, attingemus – iuro! vah! vivimus in prece!

Whooah, we're half-way there, whooah, livin' on a prayer! Take my hand, we'll make it I swear, whooah, livin' on a prayer!

Bon Jovi, *Livin' on a Prayer*

cara, tu debes mihi dicere.
ego debeam aut manere aut discedere?

Darling, you gotta let me know.
Should I stay or should I go?

The Clash, *Should I Stay or Should I Go?*

dominus cordis solius…
dominus cordis solius…
multo melius…
domino cordis infracti…

Owner of a lonely heart…
owner of a lonely heart… much better
than an owner of a broken heart…

Yes, *Owner of a Lonely Heart*

quocumque tu ambulas semper
fer tempestatem tecum…
quocumque tu ambulas semper
fer tempestatem…

Everywhere you go, always take the
weather with you…everywhere you go
always take the weather…

Crowded House, *Weather With You*

**cum excito, bene, scio me futurum
esse hominem qui excitet prope te.
cum exeo, bene, scio me futurum
esse hominem qui exeat tecum.**

When I wake up, well I know I'm gonna be,
I'm gonna be the man who wakes up next to you.
When I go out, yeah I know I'm gonna be, I'm gonna
be the man who goes along with you.

The Proclaimers, *I'm Gonna Be (500 Miles)*

**videte eas manibus iunctis ambulare
trans pontem media nocte... capita
vertuntur dum lumina fulgent – sunt
clarissima! puellae cinematographatae...
puellae cinematographatae...!**

See them walking hand in hand, across the
bridge at midnight... Heads turning as the lights flashing
out, are so bright! Girls on film... girls on film...!

Duran Duran, *Girls on Film*

**scisne te debere currere, currere,
currere, currere, currere...**

Don't you know you better run, run, run, run, run...

Tracy Chapman, *Talkin' bout a Revolution*

est oculus tigridis, est calor pugnae! surgimus ad provocationem aemuli nostri...

It's the eye of the tiger, it's the thrill of the fight! Rising up to the challenge of our rival…

Survivor, *Eye of the Tiger*

dic mihi cur dies Lunae mihi non placeant. dic mihi cur dies Lunae mihi non placeant. volo contendere totam diem.

Tell me why I don't like Mondays! Tell me why I don't like Mondays. I want to shoot the whole day down.

The Boomtown Rats, *I Don't Like Mondays*

revertite, oculi clari! huc et illuc me ruo. revertite, oculi clari! huc et illuc me ruo. est eclipsis tota cordis…

Turn around, bright eyes! Every now and then I fall apart. Turn around, bright eyes!Every now and then I fall apart. It's a total eclipse of the heart…

Bonnie Tyler, *Total Eclipse of the Heart*

tu pediseca laborabas in caupona cum ego te conveni. tu non me vis dulcis? tu non me vis?

You were working as a waitress in a cocktail bar when I met you. Don't you want me baby? Don't you want me?

The Human League, *Don't You Want Me?*

deprende has alas fractas, et disce volare iterum – disce vivere liber!

Take these broken wings, and learn to fly again – learn to live so free!

Mr Mister, *Broken Wings*

Pop
Princesses

amorem invenimus in loco exspe…
amorem invenimus in loco exspe…

We found love
in a hopeless place…
we found love in a
hopeless place…

Rihanna, *We Found Love*

**quia care, iam habemus
sanguinem malum,
scis olim fuisse amorem
insanum. vide igitur quid
tu feceris quia care iam
habemus sanguinem
malum.**

'Cause baby now we got bad blood,
you know it used to be mad love.
So take a look at what you've done,
'cause baby now we got bad blood.

Taylor Swift, *Bad Blood*

**in mea imaginatione est nulla contortio…
ego sim tam fortunata, fortunata,
fortunata, fortunata. sim tam
fortunata in amore.**

In my imagination there is no complication…
I should be so lucky, lucky, lucky, lucky.
I should be so lucky in love.

Kylie Minogue, *I Should Be So Lucky*

**omnis dies est mirabilis! tum, subito –
difficile est spirare. aliquando,
ego sum incerta doloris causa...
me tantum pudet...**

Every day is so wonderful! Then suddenly,
it's hard to breathe. Now and then, I get insecure,
from all the pain... I'm so ashamed...

Christina Aguilera, *Beautiful*

**non sum puella, sum nondum femina.
requiro modo tempus, et tempus quod
est meum, dum ego sum in medio...**

I'm not a girl, not yet a woman. All I need is time,
a moment that is mine, while I'm in between...

Britney Spears, *I'm Not a Girl, Not Yet a Woman*

**quod lusores ludent -ent, -ent, -ent, -ent,
et aspernatores oderint, -int, -int, -int -int.
care, ego modo tremam, -am,
-am, -am -am...**

'Cause the players gonna play, play, play, play, play
and the haters gonna hate, hate, hate, hate, hate.
Baby I'm just gonna shake, shake, shake, shake, shake...

Taylor Swift, *Shake it Off*

dies canum sunt completi, dies canum se finiverunt. equi veniunt igitur debes currere.

The dog days are over, the dog days are done. The horses are coming so you better run.

Florence + the Machine,
Dog Days Are Over

habeo oculum tigridis… (sum) pugnator… saltans per ignem quod sum victrix et tu audies me fremere.

I got the eye of the tiger, a fighter, dancing through the fire, 'cause I am the champion and you're gonna hear me roar.

Katy Perry, *Roar*

**sum in angulo, spectans te illam
osculari, eheu eheu! ego sum hic!
cur tu me non vides? eheu! eheu!
sed ego salto sola...**

I'm in the corner, watching you kiss her, oh oh!
I'm right over here, why can't you see me? Oh oh!
I keep dancing on my own...

Robyn, *Dancing on My Own*

**ego sum tam urbana... iam scio ego.
sum in via celeri... ab LA ad Tokyonem.**

I'm so fancy... I already know. I'm in the
fast lane... from LA to Tokyo.

Iggy Azalea (feat. Charli XCX), *Fancy*

**nix candescit in monte hac nocte,
nullum vestigium videtur...
regnum solitudinis et videtur
me reginam esse.**

The snow glows white on the mountain tonight,
not a footprint to be seen. A kingdom of isolation
and it looks like I'm the queen.

Princess Elsa, *Let It Go (Frozen)*

quandocumque, ubicumque, nos oportet coire. ero ibi erisque inibi et illud est pignus, mi amicule.

Whenever, wherever, we're meant to be together. I'll be there and you'll be near, and that's the deal my dear.

Shakira, *Whenever, Wherever*

90s Classics

quia fortasse, eris quae me servabis. et tandem... tu es meus murus mirabilis...

Because maybe, you're gonna be the one that saves me. And after all... you're my wonderwall...

Oasis, *Wonderwall*

ebria videor sed sobria sum;
iuvenis et pauper sum.
defessa sum sed laboro, euge!…
quod habeo unam manum
in meo sinu et altera
dat signum pacis.

I feel drunk but I'm sober, I'm young
and I'm underpaid. I'm tired but
I'm working, yeah!… 'Cause I've got
one hand in my pocket and
the other one is giving a peace sign.

Alanis Morissette, *Hand in My Pocket*

o! pone tuas manus…
in meam spem. curre tuis
digitis per animum meum…
pone tuas manus,
pone tuas manus!

Oh place your hands, on my hope.
Run your fingers through my soul…
put your hands on, put your hands on!

Reef, *Place Your Hands*

et per omnia, illa mihi offert praesidium, multum amorem et multam caritatem, seu ego sim iustus seu falsus.

And through it all, she offers me protection, a lot of love and affection, whether I'm right or wrong.

Robbie Williams, *Angels*

mille milibus carminibus post, et hic sum et conor tibi dicere me curare. mille milibus carminibus post, et hic sum.

A million love songs later, and here I am trying to tell you that I care. A million love songs later, and here I am.

Take That, *A Million Love Songs*

sunt septem horae et quindecim dies ex quo sustulisti amorem. exeo quaque nocte et dormio per diem, ex quo sustulisti amorem.

It's been seven hours and fifteen days since you took your love away. I go out every night and sleep all day, since you took your love away.

Sinead O'Connor, *Nothing Compares to You*

transivi limen ab furore ad sanitatem miliens et tum reversa sum. te amo, care... ego sum in catenis! ego sum in catenis!

I've crossed the line, from mad to sane, a thousand times and back again. I love you baby... I'm in chains! I'm in chains!

Tina Arena, *Chains*

non secunda est, septem secundis procul sunt… dum maneam, exspectabo. exspectabo.

It's not a second,
seven seconds away…
just as long as I stay,
I'll be waiting.
I'll be waiting.

Neneh Cherry, *7 Seconds*

ille bibit sucum cervisiae, bibit sucum sicerae. cantat carmina quae illi revocant antiquitatem, cantat carmina quae revocant aetatem optimam.

He drinks a lager drink, he drinks a cider drink. He sings the songs that remind him of the good times, he sings the songs that remind him of the best times.

Chumbawamba, *Tubthumping*

scio quid velim et id volo iam. te volo quod ego sum Dominus Vanus. scio quid velim et id volo iam. te volo quod ego sum D. Vanus.

I know what I want and I want it now. I want you, 'cause I'm Mr Vain. I know what I want and I want it now. I want you, 'cause I'm Mr. Vain.

Culture Beat, *Mr. Vain*

habes me amicum... cum via appareat difficilis prorsum et tu es longe ab lecto delicato calido...

You've got a friend in me... when the road looks rough ahead and you're miles and miles from your nice, warm bed...

Randy Newman, *You've Got a Friend in Me*

rhythmus saltator est… est comes animi… potest id sentire ubique…

Rhythm is a dancer… it's a soul's companion… you can feel it everywhere…

Snap, *Rhythm is a Dancer*

Swinging 60s

tum ego vidi eius vultum... nunc ego credo! certe non est ulla dubitatio in mea mente. ego amo et ego credo!

Then I saw her face...
now I'm a believer!
Not a trace of doubt
in my mind. I'm in love,
I'm a believer!

The Monkees, *I'm a Believer*

**ego non scio nimium de historia,
ego non scio nimium de biologia...
sed ego scio me te amare,
et scio, si tu me ames quoque -
qualem mundum!**

Don't know much about history,
dont know much biology...
but I do know that I love you, and
I know that if you love me too, what a
wonderful world this would be!

Sam Cooke, *(What a) Wonderful World*

**femina pulchra, ambulans per viam.
femina pulchra - species quam
amo convenire. femina pulchra,
ego tibi non credo tu
non es veritas...**

Pretty woman, walking down the street.
Pretty woman - the kind I like to meet.
Pretty woman, I don't believe you,
you're not the truth...

Roy Orbison, *Pretty Woman*

**omnem diem et omnem noctem.
omnem diem et omnem noctem. puella
volo esse tecum, omne tempus.**

All day and all of the night. All day and all of the night.
Girl, I want to be with you all of the time.

The Kinks, *All Day and All of the Night*

**dies Lunae, dies Lunae…
tam secunda mihi. mane die Lunae…
fuit quam sperabam futuram esse.**

Monday, Monday… so good to me.
Monday morning, it was all
I hoped it would be.

The Mamas & The Papas, *Monday Monday*

**natus sum prope flumen in paulo
tabernaculo et similis fluminis,
curro diutissime.**

I was born by the river in a little tent,
oh and just like the river I've been
running ever since.

Sam Cooke, *A Change is Gonna Come*

Motown
Maestros

inspecta propius et facile videbis vestigia lacrimarum mearum.

If you look closer,
it's easy to trace
the tracks of
my tears.

Smokey Robinson, *The Tracks of My Tears*

**desiste! in nomine amoris,
antequam tu frangas
meum cor. volve hoc
in tua mente...**

Stop! In the name of love,
before you break my heart.
Think it over...

The Supremes,
Stop! In the Name of Love

**noli culpare solem,
noli culpare lumen lunae.
noli culpare bona
tempora - culpa saltatum!**

Don't blame it on the sunshine,
don't blame it on the moonlight.
Don't blame it on the good times -
blame it on the boogie!

The Jackson 5,
Blame It on the Boogie

id me deprehendit, debeo dicere, cum cognovissem heri. tu non scis me audivisse per vitem?

It took me by surprise, I must say,
when I found out yesterday.
Don't you know that I heard it
through the grapevine?

Marvin Gaye,
I Heard It Through the Grapevine

care, care... care noli me deserere... o te obsecro, noli me deserere... solam...

Baby, baby... baby don't leave me.
Oooh please don't leave me,
all by myself...

The Supremes,
Where Did Our Love Go?

Rock n Roll

feri me,
feri me,
feri me
baculo tuo
rhythmi!

Hit me, hit me,
hit me with your
rhythm stick!

Ian Dury & The Blockheads,
Hit Me with Your Rhythm Stick

**risi amorem quod
credebam illum ridiculum esse.
advenisti et me adfecisti
cara...vah! vah!
magnas spheras ignis!**

I laughed at love 'cause I thought
it was funny. You came along and
moved me honey...
Goodness gracious, great balls of fire!

Jerry Lee Lewis, *Great Balls of Fire*

**(clama!) iactem meas
manus et clamem!
(clama!) agitem meum
caput et clamem!
age nunc, clama!**

Shout! Throw my hands up and shout!
Throw my head back and shout!
Come on now, shout!

The Isley Brothers, *Shout*

**Graecia (sic) est verbum,
tenet modum, tenet sententiam.
Graecia est tempus, est locus,
est motus. Graecia est
quomodo sentimus!**

Grease is the word, is the groove,
is the feeling. Grease is the time,
is the place, is the motion.
Grease is the way we are feeling!

Frankie Valli, *Grease*

**puellae puberes non
adlacrimant, puellae puberes
non adlacrimant. illae non
ad-ad-adlacrimant…
mea puella dixit 'vale!'**

Big girls don't cry, big girls don't cry.
They don't cry-ay-ay…
my girl said 'bye!'

Frankie Valli & the Four Seasons, *Big Girls Don't Cry*

Ratpack

quam felix unus vir esse potest! illam basiavi et me basiavit…

How lucky can one guy be! I kissed her and she kissed me…

Dean Martin, *Ain't That a Kick in the Head*

id vita est...
id est quod omnes dicunt.
habes bona tempora
in Aprili, es
concisus in Maio...

That's life...
that's what all the people say.
You're riding high in April,
shot down in May...

Frank Sinatra, *That's Life*

cognovi virum -
Boiangulum - et tibi
saltabat in
calceis attritis...

I knew a man -
Bojangles - and he'd
dance for you,
in worn-out shoes...

Sammy Davis Jnr, *Mr Bojangles*

castaneae tostae in igne... Jacobus Pruinosus mordens nasum...

Chestnuts roasting on an open fire... Jack Frost nipping at your nose...

Nat King Cole, *The Christmas Song (Chestnuts Roasting on an Open Fire)*

Rap &
Hip Hop

tu es nihil praeter fossorem auri... tu deprehendis meam pecuniam. iam sum egens.

You ain't nothin' but a gold digger... you take my money. Now I'm in need.

Kanye West (feat. Jamie Foxx), *Gold Digger*

**et cara, est mirabile,
me esse in ambage tecum.
sed non possum tuum
ludum solvere...**

And baby, it's amazing, I'm in this
maze with you. I just can't
crack your code...

Jay Z (feat. Justin Timberlake), *Holy Grail*

**videtur esse mihi negotium,
igitur omnes - me sequimini!
quod debemus habere
parvam contraversiam,
quod videtur esse
vanum sine me.**

Now this looks like a job for me
so everybody, just follow me!
'Cause we need a little controversy,
'Cause it feels so empty without me.

Eminem, *Without Me*

**veni saltare -tare, -tare, -tare.
me iactavi ad solum quod
sunt mea consilia, consilia,
consilia, consilia...**

I came to dance, dance, dance, dance.
I hit the floor, 'cause that's my
plans, plans, plans, plans…

Taio Cruz, *Dynamite*

**quia sum laetus...
plaude si tu es similis
conclavis sine trabe.
quia sum laetus... plaude
si tu credis felicitatem
veritatem esse.**

Because I'm happy…
Clap along if you feel like
a room without a roof.
Because I'm happy…
Clap along if you feel like
happiness is a truth.

Pharrell Williams, *Happy*

Teen Idols

ego non possum vultum meum sentire cum ego sum tecum. sed id amo, sed id amo…

I can't feel my face when I'm with you.
But I love it,
but I love it oh…

The Weeknd, *Can't Feel My Face*

tu eras sol meus,
tu eras mundus meus.
sed sum certus te non scivisse
omnes modos quibus te amarem.
lacrima mihi flumen.

You were my sun, you were my Earth.
But I bet you didn't know all the
ways I loved you, no. Cry me a river.

Justin Timberlake, *Cry Me a River*

desiste! mane unum momentum.
reple meum poculum, funde
vinum mihi... tu non mihi credis?
modo specta! sum nimis flagrans
(euge!), appellavi custodem et
vigilem. nimis flagrans (euge!).

Stop! Wait a minute.
Fill my cup, put some liquor in it…
Don't believe me? Just watch!
I'm too hot (hot damn!), called a police and
a fireman. I'm too hot (hot damn!).

Mark Ronson (feat. Bruno Mars), *Uptown Funk*

**capiam telum tibi,
ponam manum in gladium tibi.
me iaciam ante currum tibi.
cognoscis me facturum (esse) omnia tibi.**

I'd catch a grenade for you,
throw my hand on a blade for you.
I'd jump in front of a train for you.
You know I'd do anything for you.

Bruno Mars, *Grenade*

**vale vale... nolo esse stultus
tibi, solum alius lusor in
tuo ludo duplici. tu me oderis
sed non est mendacium,
cara vale vale vale.**

Bye bye... don't want to be a fool
for you, just another player
in your game for two.
You may hate me but
it ain't no lie, baby
bye bye bye.

*NSYNC, *Bye Bye Bye*

Nice
Noughties

odi has lineas obtusas! scio te id velle. odi has lineas obtusas…

I hate these blurred lines! I know you want it. I hate these blurred lines…

Robin Thicke (feat. TI, Pharrell), *Blurred Lines*

**quaesitum est: dic me quid tu putes de me?
emo meos proprios adamantes et emo meos
proprios anulos... calceos in meis pedibus,
emi! vestem quam gero, emi!**

Question! Tell me what you think about me?
I buy my own diamonds and I buy my own rings...
The shoes on my feet, I bought it!
The clothes I'm wearing, I bought it!

Destiny's Child, *Independent Women Pt. 1*

**ego sum superstes (quid!), ego non deseram
(quid!), ego non desistam (quid!),
ego laborabo durius (quid!).**

I'm a survivor (what!), I'm not goin' give up (what!), I'm
not goin' stop (what!), I'm goin' work harder (what!)

Destiny's Child, *Survivor*

**salve care, salve care, salve!
puellae dicunt, pueri dicunt...
salve care, salve care, salve!**

Hey baby, hey baby, hey! Girls say, boys say...
hey baby, hey baby, hey!

No Doubt, *Hey Baby*

**septem anni fugerunt
tam celerrime... exsuscita me
cum primum September se finiverit.**

Seven years has gone so fast...
wake me up when September ends.

Green Day, *Wake Me Up When September Ends*

**sumus homo (sic)? an sumus saltator (sic)?
et sum supplex quaerens responsum...
sumus homo? an sumus saltator?**

Are we human? Or are we dancer?
And I'm on my knees looking for the answer...
are we human? Or are we dancer?

The Killers, *Human*

**dic mihi, hic est ubi ego
abdicem omnia? pro te ego
coactus sum omnia audere.
quia scriptum est in muro...**

Tell me, is this where I give it all up?
For you I have to risk it all, because
the writing's on the wall...

Sam Smith, *Writing's On The Wall*

**censeo id esse verum, ego non sum
artifex noctis amatoriae. sed amor mihi
adhuc necesse est quod sum modo vir…**

Guess it's true, I'm not good at a one-night stand.
But I still need love 'cause I'm just a man…

Sam Smith, *Stay With Me*

**excita me cum perfectum erit, cum ero
sapientior et ero senior! prius me
reperiebam et non cognoscebam
me perditum esse…**

So wake me up when it's all over,
when I'm wiser and I'm older!
All this time I was finding myself
and I didn't know I was lost…

Avicii, *Wake Me Up*

**ego non requiro ullum monitum
bonum, ego sum iam imbecilla.**

I don't need no good advice,
I'm already wasted.

Girls Aloud, *No Good Advice*

**tu mihi commemoras puellam
quam ego olim cognovi…
video faciem eius quandocumque
ego te adspicio.**

You remind me of a girl that I once knew
See her face whenever I, I look at you

Usher, *U Remind Me*

**unum, duo, tres… mea cara non
adulterat nam illa me tantum
amat. id scio certe!**

One, two, three! My baby don't mess around
'Cause she loves me so. This I know fo sho! .

Outkast, *Hey Ya!*

**possum esse heros tuus, cara.
possum te basiare ut tuum
dolorem relevem…**

I can be your hero baby,
I can kiss away the pain…

Enrique Iglesias, *Hero*

noli accedere meum virum,
noli accedere meum puerum.
noli carpere meum virum...

Don't mess with my man, don't mess with
my boy. Get your hands off my man…

Lucy Pearl, *Don't Mess With My Man*

tu es pulchra, tu es pulchra, tu es
pulchra, verum est. vidi tuum vultum in
loco differto et nescio quid faciam...

You're beautiful, you're beautiful, you're beautiful
it's true. I saw your face in a crowded place
and I don't know what to do.

James Blunt, *You're Beautiful*

deus, deus, deus – nos adiuva!
mitte aliquid consilium ex caelo,
nam homines me cogunt
rogare: ubi est amor?

Father, father, father help us! Send some guidance
from above, 'Cause people got me, got me
questioning: Where is the love?

Black-Eyed Peas, *Where Is the Love?*